YOUR 2024 CRYPTO GUIDE

Your Simple, Easy-to-follow Manual for Making Massive Gains in the Next Crypto Bull Run, Without Missing Out + 15 Coins with 10x Potential in 2024 and Beyond

By

Clifford M. Kelly

TABLE OF CONTENT

Page is intentionally left blank

What Is A Crypto Bull Run?

A crypto bull run, also referred to as a bull cycle, occurs when cryptocurrency prices consistently increase for an extended duration. In this phase, most investors exhibit bullish sentiments, with demand surpassing supply, resulting in heightened overall market optimism. Various catalysts, including bitcoin halving, institutional investor involvement, interest rates, and innovations in the crypto industry, can instigate these bull cycles. It's crucial to acknowledge that corrective phases do occur within bull cycles, albeit being brief.

Market conditions are often gauged through price fluctuations, recognized as market cycles when enduring for an extended period.

Similar to traditional financial markets, cryptocurrency market cycles commence as investors acquire assets at lower prices, gradually driving up their value (bull cycle). As crypto prices peak, investors initiate asset sell-offs, marking the beginning of a downward trend (bear cycle). Extended periods of price increase or decrease define bull and bear market cycles. Notably, market cycles consist of four phases: accumulation, markup (bull run), distribution, and markdown (bear run). This cyclic pattern has been observed multiple times in Bitcoin, a key precursor to the crypto market cycle.

First Bull Run (2013)

The inaugural significant bull run for Bitcoin occurred in 2013, marked by a remarkable surge of nearly 6000 percent in its value. Starting the year at $12.5, Bitcoin soared to $754 by year-end, resulting in a crypto market capitalization of $1.2 billion. The surge in crypto prices during 2013 can be attributed to the escalating popularity of Bitcoin, a surge in transactions on crypto exchanges, and heightened demand for Bitcoin in China.

Second Bull Run (2017)

Subsequent to the 2013 bull run, Bitcoin experienced a significant decline, trading within the $300-$400 range from 2014 to 2015. This downturn was triggered by China's imposition of a comprehensive ban on crypto trading, restricting investments by Chinese individuals in cryptocurrencies.

However, Bitcoin saw a gradual recovery, reaching $500-$600 in mid-2016 and surpassing the $1000 mark by the end of the year. The pinnacle of this recovery occurred in December 2017 when prices reached $20,000, marking the second major Bitcoin bull run. Concurrently, a proliferation of crypto exchanges worldwide provided investors with opportunities to trade cryptocurrencies. The positive sentiment during this period was further fueled by the emergence of stablecoins and the growth of Ethereum's smart contract technology.

Third Bull Run (2021)

Following the 2017 bull run, Bitcoin underwent a decline and entered a markdown phase in 2018, consistently trading between $3000 and $5000 throughout the year. Various factors contributed to this bear run, including concerns about inflation and the economy, the SEC's rejection of Bitcoin ETF registration, and major digital platforms like Facebook and Google restricting ICO ads and token sales.

Despite the subdued crypto prices, technological advancements in the industry persisted. By the close of 2020, the NFT and blockchain gaming sectors emerged as significant trends. Riding on these innovations, Bitcoin prices surged to nearly

$65,000 in April 2021, marking its third major bull run.

The Present Scenario

The 2021 crypto boom lost momentum in the latter half of the year, and subdued prices persisted throughout 2022 amid deteriorating macroeconomic conditions and more stringent monetary policies. The crypto landscape experienced significant setbacks, including the decline of LUNA and the bankruptcy of prominent exchanges like FTX, Celsius, and 3AC, eroding investor confidence. Ultimately, the total crypto market capitalization plummeted from its 2021 peak of $3 trillion to $900 million in 2022.

Since early 2023, there has been a notable improvement in the crypto market. Bitcoin, starting the year just above $16,000, defied skeptics who had declared the crypto market dead and experienced a gradual increase throughout the year. By the beginning of December, it reached a 12-month high of $45,000, surprising many investors.

Ironically, Bitcoin's confidence saw a boost due to the failure of mainstream investments, including the collapse of Silicon Valley Bank (SVB). This event intensified discussions around peer-to-peer currencies and decentralization. Investors, seeking transparency after the apparent failure of traditional banking, found Bitcoin increasingly attractive as an alternative investment.

The positive momentum continued throughout the year, gaining further support with news of BlackRock's BTC exchange-traded fund (ETF) application and the subsequent surge in institutional interest in the crypto market. Bitcoin's climb from $16,000 to nearly $45,000 in a single year reflects a remarkable 180% gain, highlighting its potential resilience even in the face of significant global challenges.

What to expect from the crypto market in 2024

Bitcoin's upcoming halving event in April 2024 is a key factor signaling a potential bull market. Historically, this event, occurring roughly every four years, coincides with bullish phases in the crypto market by reducing newly minted Bitcoins, limiting supply, and sparking increased demand.

Ethereum, the second-largest cryptocurrency, is nearing the completion of its Ethereum 2.0 upgrade by the end of 2023. This upgrade promises notable enhancements in scalability, security, and energy efficiency. Features like the Shanghai upgrade and proto-dank sharding, along with staking mechanisms and transaction-burning functionalities, position Ethereum for heightened demand. The integration of zkRollups into the mainnet and the maturation of Layer-2 Ecosystems are expected to attract more stakeholders, further boosting the crypto market.

Examining broader macroeconomic trends, the positive market environment from October 2023 is influenced by global liquidity conditions. The potential Federal Reserve rate cuts in early 2024 and the introduction of spot ETFs are anticipated to increase investor participation and foster mainstream adoption in the crypto market. Advancements in blockchain scalability and user interface improvements bridge the gap between Web2 and Web3, facilitating widespread adoption.

In the evolving crypto landscape of 2024, various scenarios are conceivable. Bitcoin prices may surge, potentially surpassing previous all-time highs, or follow a pattern similar to 2023 with intermittent rallies and sideways movements. Market corrections could drive prices lower. Successful projects, backed by strong communities and innovative solutions, may redefine market leadership, exemplified by Solana's rise and the evolution of DeFi protocols.

The crypto sphere is poised for significant developments, including breakthrough decentralized applications (dApps), the convergence of crypto with AI and the metaverse, the maturation of crypto infrastructure, and regulatory considerations. These factors collectively contribute to the expectation of a substantial bull run, attracting more users and capital to the crypto space.

With a little more emphasis on the spot Bitcoin ETF approval which is likely to come in January, 2024, it is important to position yourself early enough for the massive transformation anticipated in the next few months, towards Bitcoin halving in April.

Alternative Coins (Altcoins)

Altcoin simply means, any other coin created after Bitcoin. After Bitcoin's creation, other coins started coming up with something to solve in the blockchain, and they also provide time utility. Which made an increase in the crypto ecosystem. Examples of altcoins are: Ethereum, Solana, Tron, Xrp, etc.

Not all altcoins have big potential like Bitcoin, though they provide utility according to their specific design, so before investing in Altcoins, a good fundamental research is necessary to know what you are investing into and the potential.

Shit Coins

Shitcoins are those highly volatile coins that pump and dump insanely with no utility or use cases. Developers of these coins mostly use them to make short term quick gains and after that, they abandon the project without further development. Investors buy shitcoins to make short time quick gains.

Always remember they are not long term projects so don't hold them for long. Make gains and let go. Don't be surprised, incoming years to come most of these trending shitcoins now will be nowhere to be found.

My top 10 altcoins for 10x gains

The coins listed below are based on my personal research. Due to some restraints, I won't be able to share details about that. However, these coins have proven to have great potential and there's very little chance of losing your investment on them. The good thing is, you can find all of them on Binance exchange.

Com: It's the second solid BRC20 project after $ORDI.

Hxxh: Aside $COM, this project is the second great utility project on the BTC Ordinals ecosystem.

Hook: It is a Web3 giant project with so many utilities.

Bake

Dodo

Quick

Waves

Auction

Pivx

Data

My top 5 meme coins for over 10x gains

I hope you recall what I shared about shitcoins in the previous chapter. Please put it in mind. The following meme coins are my top investments ahead of the bull run.

Meme: A meme coin backed by Binance

Coq inu: The number one meme coin on the avalanche chain.

Bonk: A solana meme coin

Doge: Backed by Elon Musk

Pepe

How to not lose your money to the market

The first thing to ensure in crypto investment is the protection of your capital. And this is by setting your stop point. This means that you must have it in mind that, if your investment goes down a particular percentage (e.g. 25% from the entry point), you'll close the trade.

Aside from securing your capital, another very important thing is to know how to take profit. I'll explain it below.

I have been in your shoe several times.

Where you enter a trade and suddenly it enters into profits but because it hasn't hit your target, while holding.

All of a sudden, the market reverses taking both the profit you made as well as a part of your capital.

This puts an end to that.

By the way, I will share with you also, the trading rules in bear market.

But for now, let's talk about why you're here.

As a crypto trader or investor, the second thing you'll learn after you've learnt how to take entries on signals when called is how to take profit.

In crypto, take profit isn't just clicking on the sell button.

Just like sometimes buying isn't just hitting the buy button.

Sometimes to buy, you've got to DCA (Dollar Cost Averaging) with several entries.

Also, sometimes, you've got to enter the trade setting a take profit and stop loss.

You have got to learn how to place orders at a given entry if the asset is yet to visit that entry.

That same way, if you want to sell, taking profit is a skill.

Reason because the market doesn't move in a straight line up trend, so also it doesn't move in a straight line downward trend.

As such, you have to learn how to take profit.

Profit is not yet yours until it's seating in a stable coin.

Sometimes, the market movement might demand you sell everything, other times, it might demand you take your capital, while some other times it might demand you take your profits.

Below are 5 strategies to help you secure your profits:

(1) Trail your Profit - this is when you move your stoploss from entry a step further where you spot a support or consolidation during an upward trend or growth.

(2) Sell off everything into a stable coin - this happens when your Profit target is hit or you feel you're good at current Profit.

(3) Sell off your capital and leave your Profit to run - this is when you want to safeguard your capital in the event the trade still has the potential of an Uptrend. It's a no risk trade.

(4) Take your Profit and leave your capital to run - this is when you are sure that your capital is safe no matter the direction of the market. Mostly applied when you take profit and move your stoploss to entry to safeguard your capital.

(5) Sell 50% of the entire holding and keep holding 50% - this is applied when you still have intention to hold for long term so that even if you lose the 50% you left, you didn't lose anything.

You have to understand when each of the profit taking strategies is the best action.

However, there might be times you don't need to set a profit target.

There is such a thing as "open trade".

Open trade is when you take entry on a trade with stoploss but no take profits target.

You can apply this kind of trade when you're not sure the price whales might pump the coin to.

But not often advised as that's a greedy approach.

In conclusion, take profit.